JEWELRY *for the* STARS

Rock the red-carpet look with 13 designs that are big on glitz and glamour.
Tease with tassels, make your point with spikes, or bring on the bling!

3

4

5

7

9

12

15

18

21

23

25

28

Be sure to read General Instructions on pages 30-32 before making your project.

LEISURE ARTS, INC. • Maumelle, Arkansas

Antique Brass Chandelier
Faceted Gold Drop
Silver Dangle

Shopping List

- ☐ 4" antique brass medium chain
- ☐ 12" antique brass fine chain
- ☐ 16 4mm teal beads
- ☐ 2 antique brass 8-hole chandelier connectors
- ☐ 2 antique brass ear wires
- ☐ 16 antique brass eye pins
- ☐ 4 4mm antique brass jump rings
- ☐ round-nose pliers
- ☐ chain-nose pliers (2 pair)
- ☐ wire cutters

To make each Antique Brass Chandelier Earring:

1. Use one eye pin and one bead to make a bead connector. Make eight bead connectors.
2. Cut eight 5/8" long pieces of fine chain. Opening one loop on the bead connector, attach one chain length to each bead connector.
3. Open the opposite loop on one bead connector. Attach one bead connector to one hole on the 8-hole connector. Repeat with the remaining bead connectors.
4. Cut a 2" length of medium chain. Use jump rings to attach the chain ends to the holes on the 8-hole connector.
5. Opening the loop on one ear wire, attach the ear wire to the center of the medium chain length.

Shopping List

- ☐ 2 12mm x 25mm gold 3-hole filigree connectors
- ☐ 12 8mm x 12mm faceted gold teardrop beads
- ☐ 12 gold eye pins
- ☐ 2 gold or antique brass ear wires
- ☐ round-nose pliers
- ☐ chain-nose pliers (2 pair)
- ☐ wire cutters

To make each Faceted Gold Drop Earring:

1. To make a double-bead dangle, thread a bead on an eye pin. Make a wrapped loop, attaching the bead dangle through one hole on one connector. Thread another bead on a second eye pin. Make a wrapped loop, attaching the bead dangle through the eye of the previous bead dangle.

2. Repeat Step 1 to make a double-bead dangle for each of the remaining holes on the connector.

3. Attach the ear wire to the top of the connector.

Shopping List

- ☐ 2 5mm x 7mm silver spacer beads
- ☐ 4 6mm silver pearl beads
- ☐ 18-gauge silver wire
- ☐ 2 silver ear wires
- ☐ chain-nose pliers (2 pair)
- ☐ round-nose pliers
- ☐ wire cutters

To make each Silver Dangle Earring:

1. Cut a 4" length of wire.

2. Center two pearl beads and a spacer bead on the wire. At each end of the beads, bend each wire end up to form a triangle *(Fig. 1)*. About 3/4" from each corner, tightly wrap one wire around the other; trim one wire end close to the wrap.

3. Cut the remaining wire end about 3/8" above the wrap and make a loop *(Fig. 2)*.

Fig. 1

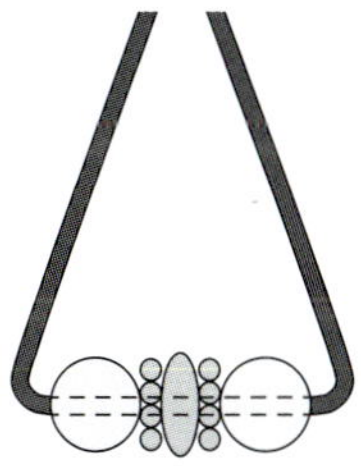

Fig. 2

4. Attach the loop to an ear wire.

Flower Necklace

Shopping List

- ☐ 3 3" diameter coral silk or polyester flowers with felt backing
- ☐ 3/4" diameter rhinestone button
- ☐ 5/8" diameter rhinestone slider
- ☐ 81 8mm white pearls
- ☐ 4 4mm white pearls
- ☐ large silver toggle clasp
- ☐ 49-strand/.018 bead stringing wire
- ☐ 8 2mm silver crimp beads
- ☐ 4 8mm silver jump rings
- ☐ coral sewing thread to match flowers
- ☐ hand sewing needle
- ☐ 1.5mm hole punch
- ☐ chain-nose pliers (2 pair)
- ☐ wire cutters
- ☐ crimp tool

Finished length: approximately 19"

To make the Necklace:

1. Thread the needle with sewing thread; knot the ends together. Sew three large pearls to the center of one flower; knot the thread on the back. In the same manner, sew the button and slider to the remaining flowers.

2. Slightly overlapping the petals, arrange 3 flowers in a curved shape. Sew the felt backings together *(Fig. 1)*.

Fig. 1

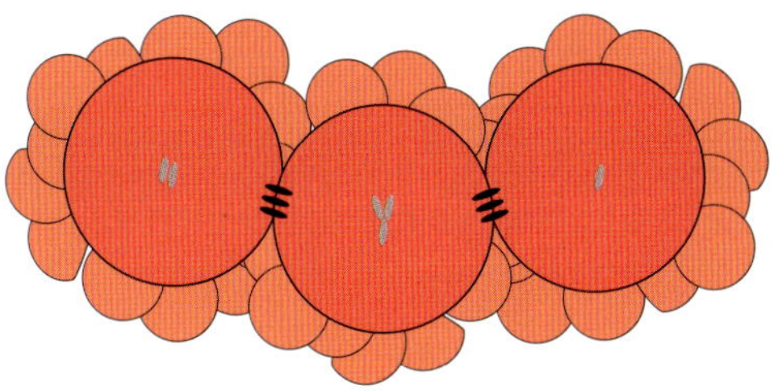

3. Punch two holes, approximately 3/8" apart, in the outer edge of the felt backing of the outer flowers *(Fig. 2)*. Attach a jump ring to each hole.

Fig. 2

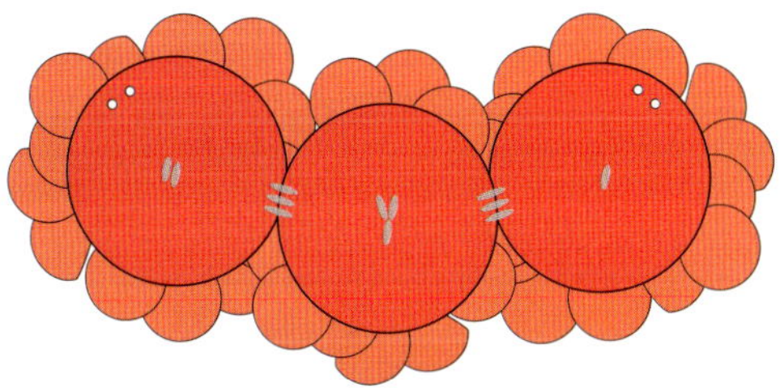

4. Cut a 10" length of stringing wire. Use a crimp bead to attach the wire to the upper jump ring on one flower. Thread 19 large pearls and one small pearl on the string. Use a crimp bead to attach the wire to one clasp piece. Repeat to attach 19 large pearls and one small pearl to the upper jump ring on the opposite flower.

5. Repeat Step 4 to thread and attach 20 large pearls and one small pearl to the lower jump ring on each flower and the remaining clasp piece, being careful not to allow the pearl strands to cross.

Rhinestone Cuff with Tassel

Shopping List

- [ ] 5-7 1" square rhinestone sliders
- [ ] 2- or 3-hole gunmetal bracelet latch clasp
- [ ] gunmetal crown charm
- [ ] 6mm gunmetal rhinestone spacer bead
- [ ] 6mm gunmetal jump ring (used as a spacer)
- [ ] 9mm grey pearl
- [ ] silver ball head pin
- [ ] 2 4mm silver jump rings
- [ ] 7mm silver jump ring
- [ ] 4 silver crimp beads
- [ ] 4 silver crimp bead covers
- [ ] $2^{1}/_{2}$" x $1^{1}/_{2}$" piece of black leather
- [ ] $1^{1}/_{2}$" length of $^{1}/_{8}$" wide black suede cord
- [ ] 49-strand/.018 bead stringing wire
- [ ] E-6000® Industrial Strength Adhesive
- [ ] clothespin
- [ ] colored pencil that will show on black leather
- [ ] chain-nose pliers (2 pair)
- [ ] round-nose pliers
- [ ] wire cutters
- [ ] crimp tool

To make the Cuff:

1. Place the sliders and clasp side-by-side on a flat surface until they measure your desired bracelet length. The bracelet can be lengthened or shortened by approximately 1" by adding or removing a slider.

2. Cut two 12" lengths of stringing wire. Use crimp beads to attach the wires to the upper and lower holes on one clasp piece. Insert the strands through the upper and lower holes on the back of the sliders. Keeping the sliders tight, use crimp beads to attach the stringing wires to the upper and lower holes on the remaining clasp piece. Attach the crimp bead covers.

3. On the wrong side of the leather, use the colored pencil to draw a line $^{1}/_{2}$" from one long edge of the leather piece ***(Fig. 1)***.

Fig. 1

4. Using scissors, cut approximately 1/8" wide strips up to the 1/2" mark *(Fig. 2)*.

Fig. 2

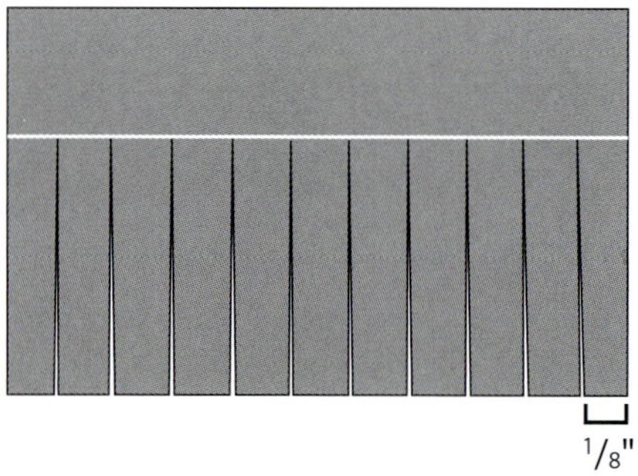

5. Fold the suede cord in half and adhere it to the upper right corner on the wrong side of the leather rectangle, leaving 1/2" of the loop hanging over the top edge *(Fig. 3)*. Apply adhesive to the upper edge on the wrong side of the leather rectangle. Roll the cut leather rectangle into a tassel. Secure the roll with the clothespin; allow to dry.

Fig. 3

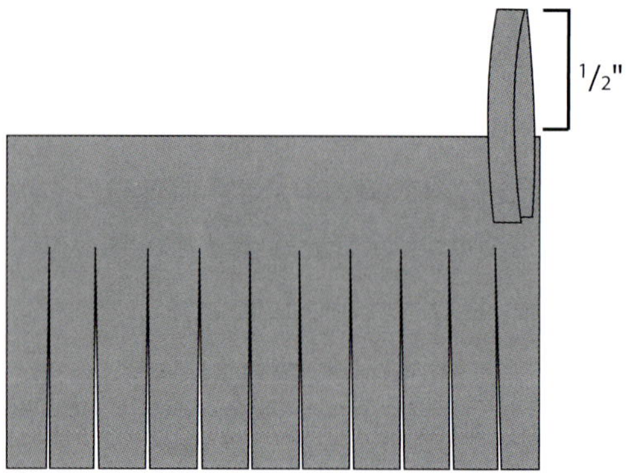

6. Thread a grey pearl, gunmetal jump ring, and rhinestone spacer bead on the head pin to make a bead dangle. Make a wrapped loop, attaching the head pin to a small silver jump ring. Use a small silver jump ring to attach the crown charm to the jump ring on the bead dangle.

7. Use the large silver jump ring to attach the tassel loop and jump ring on the charm/bead dangle to one hole on one side of the clasp.

Clay Oval Tassel Necklace

Shopping List

- ☐ Fimo® Professional oven-hardening modeling clay - fuchsia
- ☐ 30" gold medium chain
- ☐ 16" gold fine chain
- ☐ 1 1/4" gold spike charm
- ☐ 8mm gold rhinestone spacer bead
- ☐ 3 gold eye pins
- ☐ 8mm gold jump ring
- ☐ 4 4mm gold jump rings
- ☐ gold lobster clasp
- ☐ metallic gold acrylic paint
- ☐ liquid clear sealer
- ☐ small paintbrush
- ☐ micro-fine glitter
- ☐ craft knife
- ☐ glass baking dish or cookie sheet
- ☐ acrylic clay roller or clay-dedicated rolling pin
- ☐ deck of playing cards
- ☐ aluminum foil
- ☐ wax paper
- ☐ tracing paper
- ☐ E-6000® Industrial Strength Adhesive
- ☐ chain-nose pliers (2 pair)
- ☐ wire cutters

Finished length: approximately 31", excluding pendant.

To make the Necklace:

1. To condition the clay, break off half the block and use your hands to roll the clay into a ball. Flatten the ball slightly and fold it over on itself; re-roll the clay into a ball and repeat until the clay is soft and pliable.

2. Place two stacks of cards, each 18 cards high, on wax paper. Slightly flatten the clay ball and place it between the two stacks. With the clay roller riding on the stacks, roll over the clay until it is flattened.

3. Trace the oval pattern onto tracing paper; cut out. Place the pattern on the clay and use the craft knife to cut out a clay oval. Use your fingers to gently smooth and round the top edge.

4. Trim two eye pins about 1/2" from the eye. Gently insert the eye pins into the top and bottom center of the oval.

5. Follow the manufacturer's instructions to bake the oval; allow to cool.

6. Gently pull the eye pins out of the oval. Brush gold paint on the sides of the oval; allow to dry. Brush one coat of clear sealer over the entire piece; allow to dry. Brush on a second coat of clear sealer and lightly sprinkle with micro-fine glitter; allow to dry. Brush on a third coat of clear sealer; allow to dry.

7. Dip the end of each eye pin in adhesive and reinsert into the oval; allow to dry.

8. Use an eye pin and the rhinestone spacer bead to make a bead connector. Open the eye pin and attach the bead connector to one loop on the oval; close. Use two 4mm jump rings to attach the spike charm to the same loop. Cut five 3" lengths of fine chain. Open the remaining loop on the bead connector and attach the chain lengths; close the loop.

9. Find the center of the larger chain and use a 4mm jump ring to attach the clay pendant to the chain center. Use a 4mm jump ring to attach the clasp to one end of the chain. Attach the 8mm jump ring to the opposite end of the chain.

Some tips for using polymer clay

- Begin with clean hands and a clean work surface. Cover your work surface with wax paper.
- Do not ingest clay.
- It is best to use clay-dedicated tools.
- Never place unbaked clay on unprotected furniture, counter tops, or food prep surfaces.
- Use a glass baking dish or a metal pan or cookie sheet. If you are using a clay dedicated dish or pan, you can place the clay directly on the surface. Any dishes or pans that may be used later for food should be covered with aluminum foil.
- Do not use a microwave oven.
- For best results, check the oven temperature with an oven thermometer. Never exceed the recommended oven temperature.
- Follow the manufacturer's instructions for baking time. Never exceed the recommended baking time. Bake in a well-ventilated area. Baking should be completed by an adult.
- Always wash hands after handling the clay.

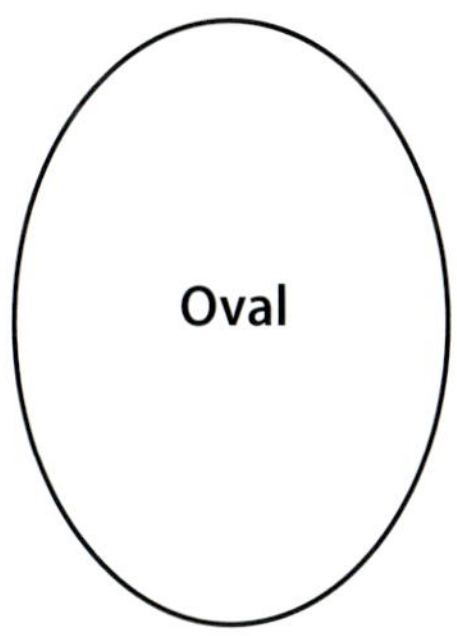

Statement Necklace

Shopping List

- ☐ 10" length of medium gold chain
- ☐ 19 8mm, 16 10mm, and 15 12mm blue faceted acrylic beads
- ☐ 6 8mm, 2 10mm, and 4 12mm aqua faceted acrylic beads
- ☐ 29 8mm gold ball beads
- ☐ 17 gold seed beads
- ☐ gold toggle clasp
- ☐ 13 gold head pins
- ☐ 9 gold eye pins
- ☐ 4 gold crimp beads
- ☐ 2 3mm gold jump rings
- ☐ 2 5mm gold jump rings
- ☐ 49-strand/.018 bead stringing wire
- ☐ spring-style bead stop
- ☐ round-nose pliers
- ☐ chain-nose pliers (2 pair)
- ☐ wire cutters
- ☐ crimp tool

Finished length: approximately 19"

To make the Necklace:

1. Cut the gold chain in half. Use a 3mm jump ring to attach one end of each chain to the toggle clasp sections. Attach a 5mm jump ring to the opposite end of each chain.

2. Use a head pin, a seed bead, and an 8mm aqua bead to make a bead dangle. Make two of these.

3. Use a head pin, a seed bead, and a 10mm blue bead to make a bead dangle. Make two of these.

4. Use an eye pin and a 10mm aqua bead to make a bead connector. Use a head pin, a seed bead, and an 8mm blue bead to make a bead dangle. Open the loop and attach the bead dangle to the eye pin on the aqua bead connector; close the loop. Make two of these.

5. Use an eye pin and a 12mm blue bead to make a bead connector. Use a head pin, a seed bead, and a 8mm aqua bead to make a bead dangle. Open the loop and attach the bead dangle to the eye pin on the blue bead connector; close the loop. Make two of these.

6. Use an eye pin and a 12mm aqua bead to make a bead connector. Use a head pin, a seed bead, and a 10mm blue bead to make a bead dangle. Open the loop and attach the bead dangle to the eye pin on the aqua bead connector; close the loop. Make two of these.

7. Use an eye pin and a 12mm blue bead to make a bead connector. Use a head pin, a seed bead, an 8mm aqua bead, and a 12mm blue bead to make a bead dangle. Open the loop and attach the bead dangle to the eye pin on the blue bead connector; close the loop. Make two of these.

8. Use an eye pin and a 12mm aqua bead to make a bead connector. Use a head pin, a seed bead, a 12mm blue bead, and a 12mm aqua bead to make a bead dangle. Open the loop and attach the bead dangle to the eye pin on the aqua bead connector; close the loop.

Refer to the photo on page 14 for Steps 9-12.

9. Cut two 13" lengths of stringing wire. Use a crimp bead to attach the wires to one 5mm jump ring on a chain length. Thread one seed bead and four 12mm blue beads on ***both*** wire lengths. Threading the bead dangles between the beads as shown, thread one 8mm blue bead, twelve 10mm blue beads and one 8mm blue bead on ***one*** wire length. Place the bead stop on the end of the wire.

10. Thread one seed bead, fifteen 8mm blue beads, and one seed bead on the remaining wire length.

11. Thread four 12mm blue beads, and one seed bead on ***both*** wire lengths. Use a crimp bead to attach the wire to the 5mm jump ring on the remaining chain.

12. Cut a 13" length of stringing wire. Use a crimp bead to attach the wire to the chain about $^{3}/_{8}$" above the 5mm jump ring on one side. Thread the gold ball beads on the wire length. Use a crimp bead to attach the beaded strand about $^{3}/_{8}$" above the 5mm jump ring on the opposite side.

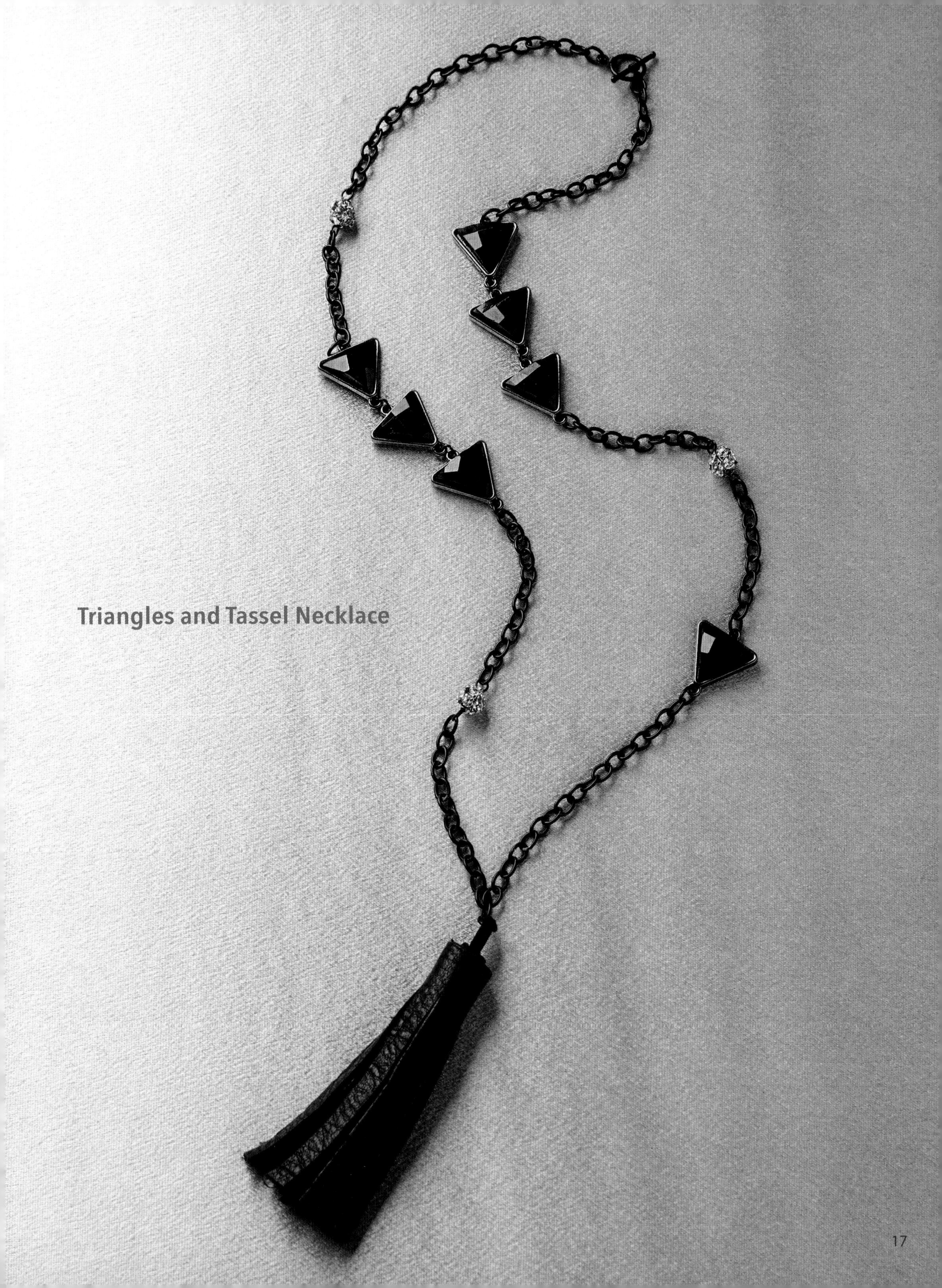

Triangles and Tassel Necklace

Shopping List

- ☐ 2 1/2" x 3" piece of black leather
- ☐ 1 1/2" length of 1/8" wide black suede cord
- ☐ 23" length of black chain
- ☐ 18mm black faceted triangle connector strand (7 triangles)
- ☐ 3 8mm rhinestone spacer beads
- ☐ 3 black eye pins
- ☐ black toggle clasp
- ☐ 4 4mm black jump rings
- ☐ 6mm black jump ring
- ☐ E-6000® Industrial Strength Adhesive
- ☐ colored pencil that will show on black leather
- ☐ clothespin
- ☐ chain-nose pliers (2 pair)
- ☐ round-nose pliers
- ☐ wire cutters

Finished length: approximately 29", excluding tassel.

To make the Necklace:

1. On the wrong side of the leather, use the colored pencil to draw a line 1/2" from one short edge of the leather piece *(Fig. 1)*.

Fig. 1

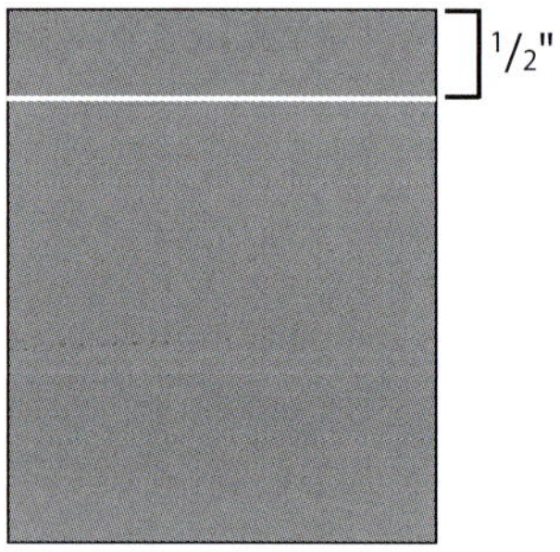

2. Using scissors, cut approximately 1/8" wide strips up to the 1/2" mark *(Fig. 2)*.

Fig. 2

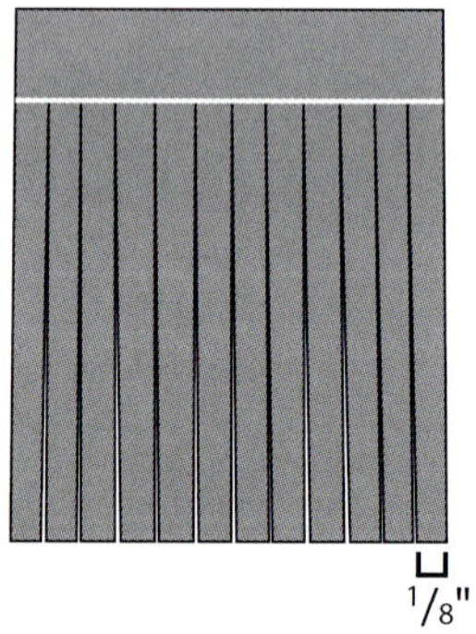

3. Fold the suede cord in half and adhere it to the upper right corner on the wrong side of the leather rectangle, leaving 1/2" of the loop hanging over the top edge *(Fig. 3)*. Apply adhesive to the upper edge on the wrong side of the leather rectangle. Roll the cut leather rectangle into a tassel. Secure the roll with the clothespin; allow to dry.

Fig. 3

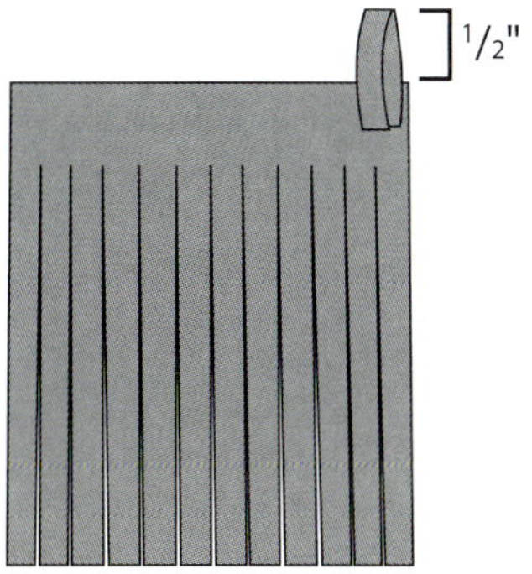

4. Use an eye pin and a rhinestone spacer bead to make a bead connector. Make a total of 3 bead connectors.

5. Take the triangle connector strand apart. Use 4mm jump rings to connect three faceted triangles together; make two sets.

6. Cut the chain into the following lengths: 5 3/4", 4", 3", 2 1/2", two 2", and 1 3/4".

7. Referring to photo (page 17), open the end links on the chain lengths to join the bead connectors, triangle sets, triangle connector, toggle clasp pieces, and chains together.

8. Use the 6mm jump ring to attach the tassel to the center of the necklace.

Spike Necklace

Shopping List

- ☐ 13 1 1/4" gold metal spike charms
- ☐ 158 3mm bronze cube beads (or 18" bead strand)
- ☐ 18" length of antique brass chain
- ☐ 5mm antique brass jump ring
- ☐ 7mm antique brass jump ring
- ☐ antique brass lobster clasp
- ☐ 2 gold crimp beads
- ☐ 49-strand/.018 bead stringing wire
- ☐ chain-nose pliers (2 pair)
- ☐ wire cutters
- ☐ crimp tool

Finished length: approximately 18", excluding spikes

To make the Necklace:

1. Cut a 23" length of stringing wire. Use a crimp bead to attach one end of the wire to the 7mm jump ring. Thread 61 cube beads onto the stringing wire. Then thread on 13 spike charms with 3 cube beads between each spike. Thread 61 more cube beads onto the stringing wire. Use a crimp bead to attach the end of the wire to the 5mm jump ring.

2. Open the 5mm jump ring. Attach one end of the chain and the clasp to the jump ring; close the jump ring.

3. Open the 7mm jump ring. Attach the opposite end of the chain to the jump ring; close the jump ring.

Multi-Strand Bracelet

Shopping List

- ☐ 9-11 10mm x 15mm turquoise nugget beads
- ☐ 13-17 6mm pink wooden round beads
- ☐ 12-16 5mm x 8mm cream barrel beads
- ☐ 62-70 3mm antique bronze cube beads
- ☐ 11-13 4mm gold disk spacer beads
- ☐ 4mm antique brass ball bead
- ☐ 6"-9" length of 10mm x 12mm antique bronze large oval link chain
- ☐ 4-ply brown waxed cord
- ☐ antique brass cross charm
- ☐ toggle clasp
- ☐ antique brass head pin
- ☐ 25-33 antique brass eye pins
- ☐ 4 5mm antique brass jump rings
- ☐ round-nose pliers
- ☐ chain-nose pliers (2 pair)
- ☐ wire cutters

To make the Bracelet:

1. To determine the finished length of the bracelet, measure wrist and subtract the length of the joined toggle clasp.

2. Cut a 12" length of cord. Tie one end of the cord to a jump ring with 3 or 4 overhand knots. Cut the excess cord and pinch the knot together tightly with your fingers. Thread a cube bead onto the cord. Alternating the beads, thread nugget beads and gold disc spacer beads onto the cord until the beaded area is approximately the length determined in Step 1. Thread another cube bead onto the cord. Tie the remaining end to a jump ring; trim and pinch the knot.

3. Use an eye pin and a wooden bead to make a bead connector. Make enough bead connectors that when joined will equal the length of the nugget bead strand. Open and close the loops to connect the bead connectors together. Attach the loop on each end to the jump rings on the nugget bead strand.

4. Cut the oval chain to the length of the nugget bead strand. Open the end links of the chain and attach them to the jump rings on the previous strands.

5. Use an eye pin and a cream barrel bead to make a bead connector. Make enough bead connectors that when joined will equal the length of the nugget bead strand. Open and close the loops to connect the bead connectors together. Attach the loop on each end to the jump rings on the previous strands.

6. Cut a 12" length of cord. Tie one end of the cord to the jump ring on the previous strands with 3 or 4 overhand knots. Cut the excess cord and pinch the knot together tightly with your fingers. Thread the remaining cube beads onto the cord until it is the same length as the other strands. Tie the remaining end to the opposite jump ring; trim and pinch the knot.

7. Use a jump ring to attach the bar end of the toggle clasp to the jump ring on the previous strands. Attach the remaining end of the toggle clasp to the opposite end in the same manner.

8. To make a bead dangle, thread a ball bead, a gold disk spacer bead, and a cream barrel bead onto the head pin. Make a wrapped loop, attaching the bead dangle to a jump ring. Attach the jump ring to the cross. Attach the jump ring to the jump ring on the previous strands.

Vintage Tassel Necklace

Shopping List

- ☐ 55 4mm antique brass ball beads
- ☐ 8 3mm bronze cube beads
- ☐ 5mm x 8mm grey rondelle bead
- ☐ 5mm rhinestone rondelle bead
- ☐ 18mm antique copper magnolia bead cap
- ☐ 5 3mm x 5mm dark orange rondelle beads
- ☐ 16" length of medium link antique brass chain
- ☐ 38" length of antique brass small chain for tassel
- ☐ 22" length of 1.5mm round leather cord
- ☐ 2 10mm antique copper jump rings
- ☐ 2 4mm antique copper jump rings
- ☐ 2 antique copper crimp beads
- ☐ 49-strand/.018" bead stringing wire
- ☐ 24-gauge antique copper wire
- ☐ 18-gauge antique copper wire
- ☐ 5 antique brass ball head pins
- ☐ round-nose pliers
- ☐ chain-nose pliers (2 pair)
- ☐ wire cutters
- ☐ crimp tool

Finished necklace: approximately 26", excluding tassel

To make the Necklace:

1. Attach a 10mm jump ring to each end of the 16" chain length.

2. Use a crimp bead to attach a 14" stringing wire length to one 4mm jump ring. Beginning and ending with 3 ball beads, thread the cube beads and ball beads on the wire, placing a cube bead after every 7 ball beads. Use a crimp bead to attach the beaded wire length to the remaining 4mm jump ring. Attach each 4mm jump ring to one 10mm jump ring.

3. Cut two 11" leather cord lengths. Holding the lengths together, thread the cord lengths through one 10mm jump ring and fold over $^1/_2$" *(Fig. 1)*. Tightly wrap an 8" length of 24-gauge wire around the folded cord 8-11 times *(Fig. 2)*. Tucking the wire ends down into the wraps, pinch the wire down with the chain-nose pliers. Trim any excess wire. Repeat with the remaining 10mm jump ring. The leather cords should be the same length as the beaded wire length.

Fig. 1

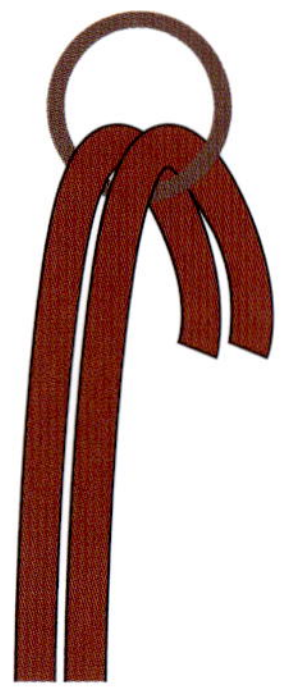

Fig. 2

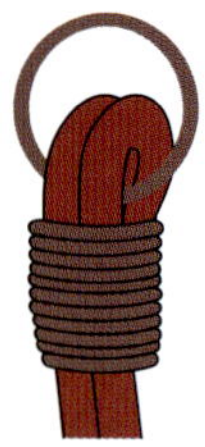

4. For the tassel, cut the small chain into 12 3" lengths. Cut a 6" length of the 18-gauge wire. Thread one end of each 3" chain length on the wire. Bend the wire into a loop (containing all 12 chain lengths) and twist the end around the wire *(Fig. 3)*.

Fig. 3

5. Thread the wire end through the bead cap, the rhinestone rondelle bead, and the grey rondelle bead. Make a wrapped loop, placing the loop over the center of the cords and the beaded strand.

6. Using the ball head pins and the dark orange rondelles, make and randomly attach wrapped bead dangles to the tassel chains.

Tassel Necklace and Earrings

Shopping List

Necklace

- ☐ 54 4mm gold ball beads
- ☐ 5 10mm gold disk beads
- ☐ $7^1/_2$" length of 10mm x 14mm gold oval chain (19 links)
- ☐ 24" length of fine gold chain
- ☐ 5 gold eye pins
- ☐ 49-strand/.018 bead stringing wire
- ☐ 4 2mm gold crimp beads
- ☐ small gold lobster clasp
- ☐ 8mm gold jump ring
- ☐ chain-nose pliers (2 pair)
- ☐ round-nose pliers
- ☐ wire cutters
- ☐ crimp tool

Earrings

- ☐ 2 gold ear wires
- ☐ 2 10mm x 14mm gold oval chain links
- ☐ 10" fine gold chain
- ☐ 2 10mm gold disk beads
- ☐ 2 gold eye pins
- ☐ chain-nose pliers (2 pair)
- ☐ round-nose pliers
- ☐ wire cutters

To make the Necklace:

1. To make a beaded tassel, thread a disk bead on an eye pin. Make a wrapped loop, attaching the eye pin to the center link on the oval chain. Cut four 1" lengths of fine chain. Open the bottom loop of the eye pin and attach the chain lengths; close the loop. Repeat to make and attach four more beaded tassels, attaching two on each side of the center tassel, skipping a chain link in between.

2. Cut 7" of stringing wire. Use a crimp bead to attach the wire to one end of the oval chain. Thread 27 ball beads on the wire. Use a crimp bead to attach the wire to the jump ring.

3. Repeat Step 2 to make and attach a beaded strand to the opposite chain end and lobster clasp.

To make each Earring:

1. To make a beaded tassel, thread a disk bead on an eye pin. Make a loop and attach the eye pin to one oval link. Cut four 1" lengths of fine gold chain. Open the bottom loop of the eye pin and attach the chain lengths; close the loop.

2. Open and close the loop to attach an ear wire to the oval link.

General Instructions

TOOLS

Chain-nose pliers have rounded, tapered jaws and a flat interior surface that will not mar wire. These pliers are used for reaching into tight places, gripping objects, opening and closing jump rings, and bending wire.

Round-nose pliers have round jaws that are useful for making loops and bending wire smoothly.

Wire cutters are used to cut small gauge wire, head pins, and eye pins.

A crimp tool (also known as crimping pliers) flattens and shapes the crimp bead or crimp tube.

Chain-nose pliers

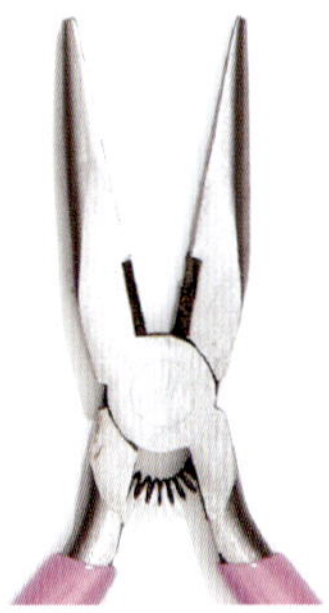

Round-nose pliers

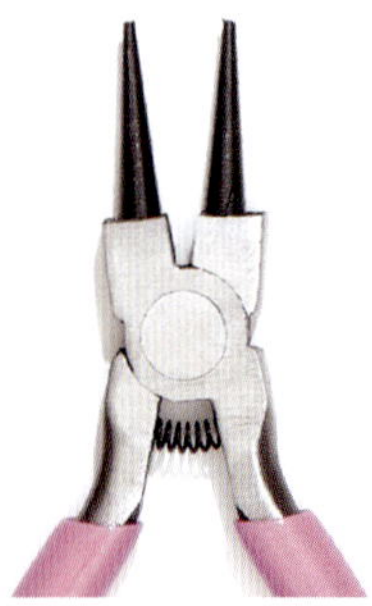

Wire cutters

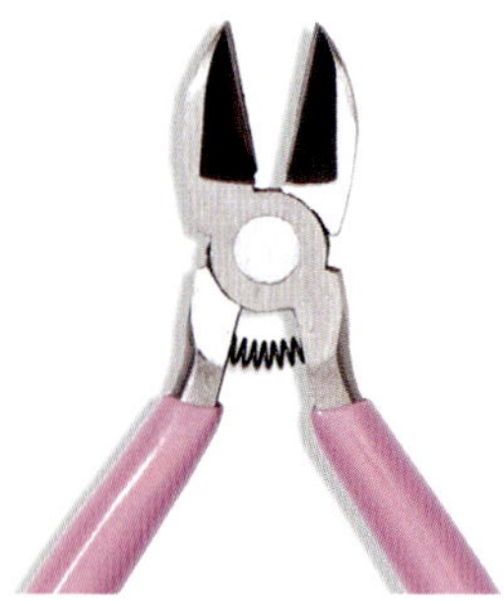

Crimp tool

TECHNIQUES

Opening and Closing Loops, Chain Links, or Jump Rings

Hold one side of the loop, link, or jump ring with chain-nose pliers. With a second pair of chain-nose pliers, gently hold the other side of the loop. Open the loop by pulling one pair of pliers toward you while pushing the other away *(Fig. 1)*.

Fig. 1

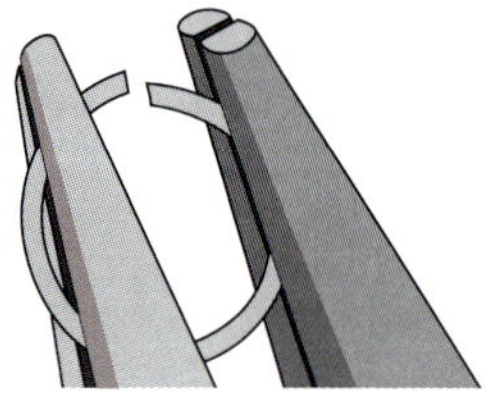

Close the loop by pushing and pulling the pliers in opposite directions, bringing the loop ends back together.

Making Bead Dangles and Bead Connectors

To make a bead dangle, slide the bead(s) on a head pin. Leaving about 1/2", cut off the excess wire. Using chain-nose pliers, bend the wire at a 90° angle *(Fig. 2)*. Grasp the wire end with the round-nose pliers. Turn the pliers and bend the wire into a loop *(Figs. 3-4)*. Release the pliers. Straighten or twist the loop further if necessary.

To make a bead connector, slide the bead(s) on an eye pin. Follow bead dangle instructions, above, to make a loop on the end of an eye pin.

Fig. 2

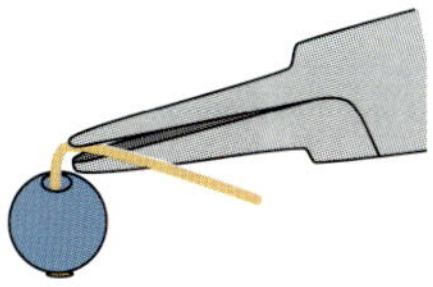

Fig. 3

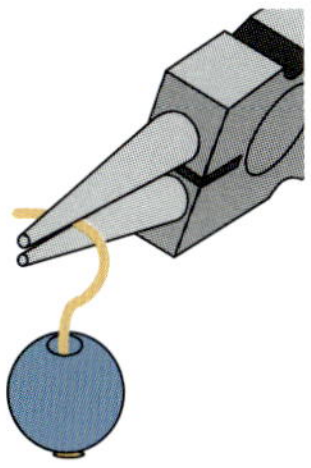

Fig. 4

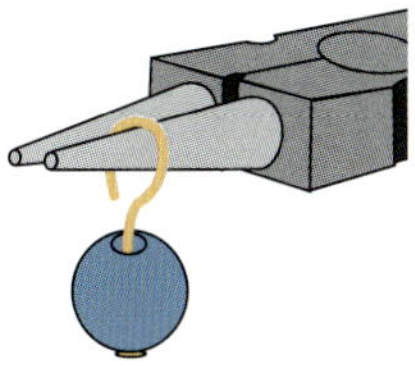

Making a Wrapped Loop on a Head Pin, Eye Pin, or Wire End

Slide the bead(s) on a head pin, eye pin, or wire end. Using chain-nose pliers, bend the wire at a 90° angle about 1/8" above the bead *(Fig. 5)*. Grasp the wire with the round-nose pliers at the 90° bend. Use your finger to push the wire around the barrel of the pliers *(Fig. 6)*. Remove the pliers. Now is the time to slide the loop onto your project or to add something to the wrapped loop. Holding the loop with the chain-nose pliers, use a second pair of chain-nose pliers to wrap the wire end around itself above the bead 3-5 times *(Fig. 7)*. Trim the excess wire and tuck the wire end into the wraps with chain-nose pliers.

Fig. 5

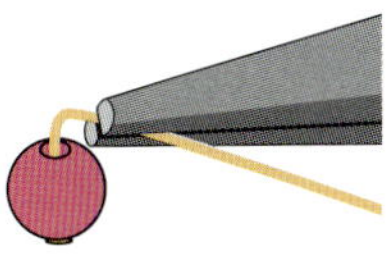

Fig. 6

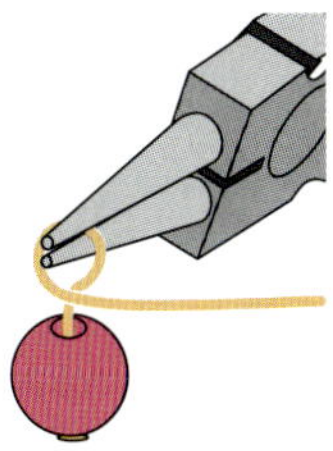

Fig. 7

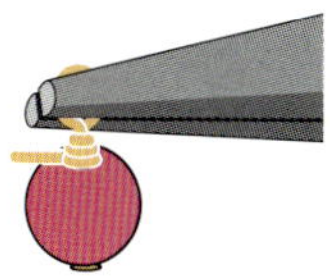

Using Crimp Beads

To finish a wire end, thread a crimp bead and the clasp or jump ring on the wire. Run the wire back through the crimp bead; use a pair of pliers to pull and tighten the wire *(Fig. 8)*. Place the crimp bead on the inner groove of the crimp tool and squeeze *(Fig. 9)*.

Release the tool, turn the crimp bead a quarter turn, and place it in the outer groove *(Fig. 10)*. Squeeze the tool to round out the crimp bead *(Fig. 11)*. Trim the wire end or if the design calls for beads, thread the beads over the wire to cover the end.

Fig. 8

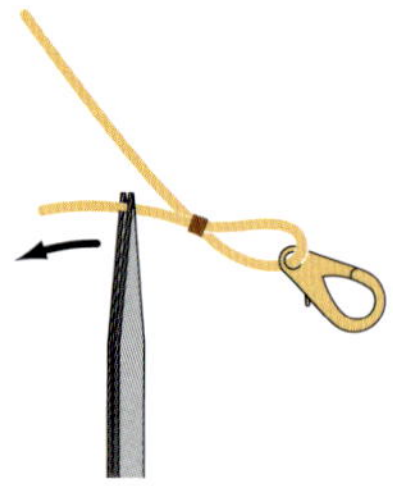

Fig. 9

Fig. 10

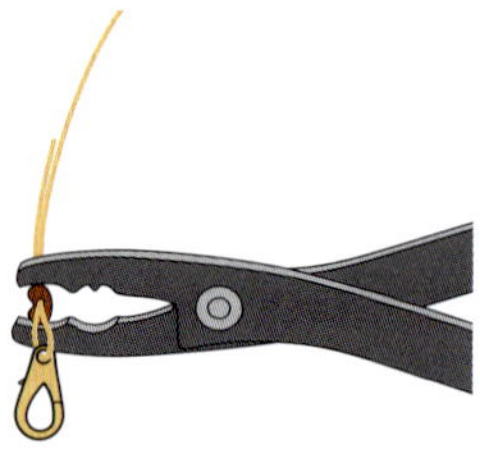

Fig. 11

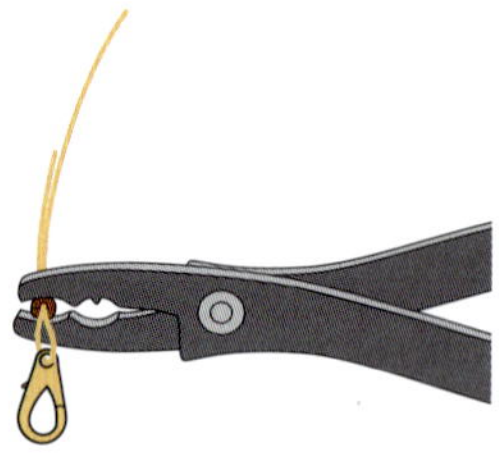

Attaching Crimp Bead Covers

If needed, use chain-nose pliers to open the crimp bead cover just enough to fit over the crimp bead. Place the crimp bead cover over the crimp bead. Use the pliers to gently squeeze the crimp cover closed, keeping the crimp cover round.

Production Team: Technical Writer – Lisa Lancaster; Technical Associate – Mary Sullivan Hutcheson; Editorial Writer – Susan Frantz Wiles; Senior Graphic Artist – Lora Puls; Graphic Artist – Cailen Cochran; Photostylists – Angela Alexander and Sondra Daniel; Photographers – Jason Masters and Ken West.